Nature's Children

CORALS

Rob Houston

GROLIER

FACTS IN BRIEF

Classification of Corals

Class: *Cnidaria* (sea anemones, corals, jellyfish, hydroids)

Subclass: *Anthozoa* (sea anemones and corals)

Order: *Scleractinia* (true or stony corals)

Species: At least 2,500 species of true or stony corals. There are also 100 kinds of black corals and thorny corals; 1,200 kinds of horny corals; and 1 kind of blue coral.

World distribution.   Corals live in oceans around the world, but mostly in tropical waters.

Habitat.   Corals live on the seabed. Most live in warm, shallow waters near coasts. Only a few live in deep oceans.

Distinctive physical characteristics.   True corals have a soft, round body with tentacles and stingers, and a stony skeleton. They live in large colonies that often form reefs.

Habits.   Stays still in its case on the seabed all its adult life.

Diet.   Corals catch passing small sea animals with stingers and tentacles. They also get sugar from algae living inside them.

© 2004 The Brown Reference Group plc
Printed and bound in U.S.A.
Edited by John Farndon and Angela Koo

Published by:

GROLIER

An imprint of Scholastic
Library Publishing
Old Sherman Turnpike, Danbury,
Connecticut 06816

Library of Congress Cataloging-in-Publication Data

Houston, Rob.
    Corals / Rob Houston.
       p. cm. — (Nature's children)
    Includes index.
    Summary: Describes the physical characteristics, habits, and natural environment of corals.
    ISBN 0-7172-5957-9 (set)   ISBN 0-7172-5961-7
     1. Corals—Juvenile literature. [1. Corals.] I. Title. II. Series.

QL377.C5H68 2004
593.6—dc22

2003049165

Contents

Coral reefs look like amazingly colorful gardens of flowers in the blue tropical sea.

Corals are small, simple animals, but they create the most stunning displays of color and wildlife in the ocean—coral reefs. Coral reefs are amazing rocklike structures found in warm, shallow seas. They are built up from the hard body cases of millions of coral animals.

Living coral reefs are home to one-quarter of all kinds of ocean creatures. Here live darting shoals of multicolored fish and a dazzling array of other creatures such as sea anemones, shrimps, sea urchins, sea slugs, sea lilies, sponges, sea squirts, and starfish. The biggest coral reef is the Great Barrier Reef off the Australian coast. It is the largest structure on Earth made by living things.

Plants or Animals?

Opposite page:
This coral cousin may look like a bouquet of flowers. In fact, it is a cluster of little animals called mat anemones.

Corals are animals, but they look a lot like plants from a distance. They don't move from place to place like other animals but remain stuck in one spot. Many corals branch like underwater trees. They form thickets of bushy growths like plants. At dusk flowerlike shapes appear and stretch out from the coral branches. But these shapes are not really flowers. They are animals with tentacles and a mouth, and something like a stomach. They extend their tentacles not to catch sunlight but to catch and eat animals.

If you mistook corals for plants, you would not be the first to do so. The world's best scientists puzzled over the nature of corals for hundreds of years. Even today the scientific name for many corals is Zoantharia, meaning "animal flowers." The group's overall name is Anthozoa, which means "flower animals."

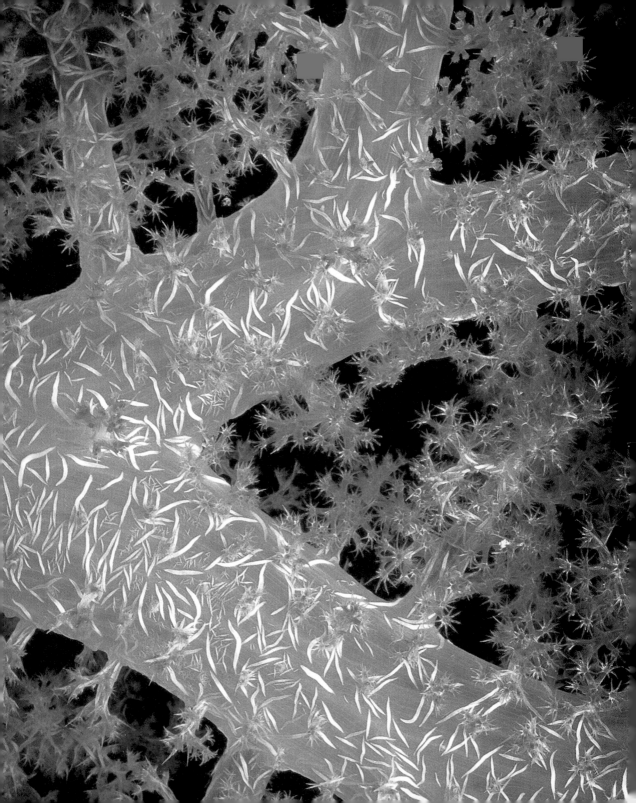

Polyps

If you could look at a branching, bushlike coral up close, you might see that it is not one individual but hundreds, thousands, or even millions of tiny individuals stuck together. The individuals are called coral polyps. They poke out of holes in the coral branches. With a magnifying lens you might be able to see a single polyp, which is usually less than a third of an inch (10 millimeters) across.

A polyp is a very simple animal. It has a cup-shaped body of two tissue layers. It is a little like a tennis ball that you have pressed hard so that it caves in. Around the rim of the cup is a ring of tentacles. The cup-shaped polyp sits in a cup-shaped hole in a branch of the coral.

These may look like the branches of a tree. In fact, they are lots of tiny animals called coral polyps, stuck together.

Building Corals

How do tiny, simple coral animals team up to make large branches and trees of coral shapes? One of the secrets is the way coral polyps make their skeleton. It is the hard structure that supports and protects the coral. The polyps take minerals out of seawater. They then use them to make a hard case around their body. By teaming up with all their neighbors, polyps can together build a large stony skeleton that protects and supports them all.

The other main secret is the way coral polyps multiply. A new baby polyp simply divides off from its parent, yet remains attached as a very close neighbor. The new polyps then divide again and again, making copies of themselves. Eventually there are a great number of polyps. They all remain attached and together form a group called a colony. The polyps in a colony are not only close neighbors—they are also identical twins, or clones.

This is a coral's skeleton, the hard structure that supports the animals as bones support your body.

Grabbing Food

Although coral polyps cannot move from place to place, they are hunters. They can hunt while sitting still because seawater is thick with drifting food. This food includes tiny creatures, dead bits of animals and plants, and animal waste. Corals catch anything that floats by but prefer animal food such as plankton. Plankton is made up of tiny algae and animals that drift on ocean currents.

Coral polyps come out to feed at night. That is when plankton drifts up from the depths and comes out from hiding places. The polyps taste the water for signs of something to eat or feel for the faint brush of an animal swimming past. As soon as the polyp senses something, it shoots out its secret weapon—stinging threads, or stingers. If the stingers hit their victim, they paralyze it. To stop the motionless animal from floating away, a coral stinger has backward-pointing hooks that hang onto the victim. The polyp then hauls its catch into its mouth with tentacles.

Opposite page:
Like flowers opening in the sun, coral polyps open up to take in food passing by in the water. These cup corals are feeding on a tiny fish.

Problem Neighbors

The stinging threads that corals use for catching food are also effective weapons. Corals are well protected inside their stony skeleton. But some animals, such as fish and starfish, still try to eat them. Coral stingers are powerful enough to paralyze tiny animals, and they can cause shock and pain to some larger animals. Some corals are particularly well armed. Fire coral has stingers that shoot out strongly enough to pierce human skin. They also have a poison that causes great pain to people if they are careless enough to brush against the coral.

Corals do not make good neighbors. They use their stingers on each other to defend their living space. The polyps on the edges of a coral colony wage war on nearby colonies if they begin to grow too close. They throw out tentacles to attack the neighboring colony's polyps. They may kill or even eat any polyps within reach. They may also send out harmful chemicals that can kill neighboring colonies.

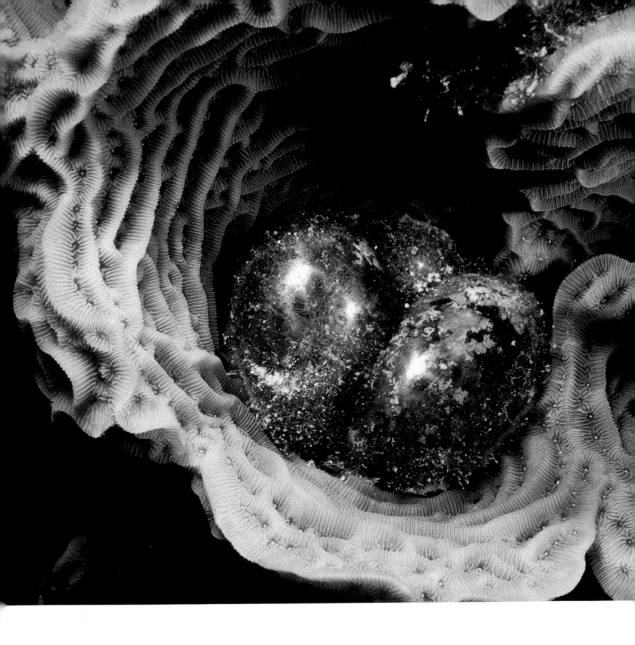

This large algae is living on a coral. Much smaller algae live inside it and help it grow.

Sun Power

Many corals do not get all their food by catching it with tentacles and stingers. Some corals get food another way too, especially corals living in shallow, sunlit water. These corals are given food by little life forms called algae that live inside their bodies.

Seaweed is a kind of algae, but most algae are much, much smaller. The algae that live in coral are so small that up to 30 million of them can live in each thimble-size polyp. Like plants, algae soak up energy from sunlight. Coral algae use the energy to make their sugary food from seawater.

Both coral and algae benefit from living together. For the algae the coral is a safe place to live. Here inside they are protected by the coral's skeleton and stingers. In return for this protection the corals get sugar from the algae. In fact, most reef corals may get three-quarters of their food from their algae. Without algae reef corals grow three times more slowly.

Antlers, Tables, and Brains

Coral polyps get a lot out of living together in colonies. In fact, some polyps live so close they can link up to other polyps with tubes or threads of body tissue. That way they can give food to one another. So when one gets too much, it can simply hand it on.

Another benefit of living together is that corals can grow into different body shapes and sizes to better cope with conditions. In places where corals are battered by waves, they form tough, stubby finger shapes. Deeper in the water it is calmer. Here corals can grow into more fragile, branched treelike or antlerlike shapes called elkhorns and staghorns. They stick out into the water and are great for picking up food. Even deeper it gets dark. The coral must catch all the sunlight it can for the algae in its body. Here corals often form wide table shapes or delicate leaflike structures to catch the glimmers of sunlight.

What Corals Like

Corals grow best in warm, bright, shallow seawater. That is why most corals live in the tropics, the warmest part of Earth. Corals hate fresh water, so no corals grow in rivers or lakes, or even anywhere near river mouths. Rivers bring sand and mud as well as fresh water. Mud is something else corals don't like. Mud clogs up coral polyps and blocks out the sunshine. So less light can shine through on the coral's vital algae.

Corals like clear, bright seawater best. Clear water does not have a lot of food in it. But the bright sunlight means the algae that live inside it provide plenty of extra food. But deeper than 150 feet (46 meters) or so down, most corals do not have algae. There it is too dark for algae to live, even in clear water. Corals here grow slowly because they have no algae to help them.

Opposite page: *Corals do best where the water is incredibly clear, like this. Clear water means the sun can penetrate to give energy to the algae the corals rely on.*

Reef Building

In warm, bright seas corals go on growing and build skeletons as they grow. Each young polyp makes its skeleton on top of the skeletons of old and dead polyps. So a coral colony builds upward and outward.

A colony may live for centuries. But in the end it stops growing and dies. The remains of all the skeletons then crumble to rocky rubble. Usually, though, new, young colonies begin to grow on top. They too will eventually die and crumble to rock. After thousands of years of growing and dying, the corals build up huge ridges of rock on the seabed called coral reefs.

Coral reefs can grow big enough to be seen from space. Over 600,000 years corals built the Great Barrier Reef off Australia. It is 1,430 miles (2,300 kilometers) long. The remains of coral skeletons can actually build dry land. The entire Bahama Islands were built by coral.

Parts of a Reef

Coral reefs usually begin growing near land. Small reefs along a coast are called fringing reefs. Typically, the reefs grow where the water is between 15 and 75 feet (5–25 meters) deep. Here the water is both calm and sunlit. Hundreds of different types of corals may live on the same bit of reef.

Fringing reefs are battered and broken by the waves. But they grow upward as the corals fight for a brightly lit spot near the water surface. Sometimes they grow up so steeply that the seaward side of the reef looks more like a wall.

Behind the growing reef ridge is the reef flat. It is a shallow area that is baked by the sun so strongly that few corals can live there. Sometimes it is worn away to form a lagoon, and the coral reef becomes a barrier reef separated from the land.

Homes and Hiding Places

Opposite page: *Coral reefs provide great hiding places for a host of creatures like this moray eel, poking its head out of a crack.*

Coral reefs are truly marvels of the natural world. They are a home for one-quarter of all kinds of sea creatures. What makes reefs so attractive for sea creatures is the way corals team up with algae to make food from sunlight. The food created by algae feeds not only the corals but the whole community of animals. Some animals get the sugar by eating coral. Other animals benefit by eating the animals that feed on the coral.

Coral also builds intricate shapes on the seabed. These shapes provide lots of nooks and crevices for animals to hide in and make themselves at home. Everything from shrimps to octopuses and ferocious moray eels hide in holes made by coral skeletons. Outside, shoals of brightly colored fish move in to lurk, waiting for things to emerge.

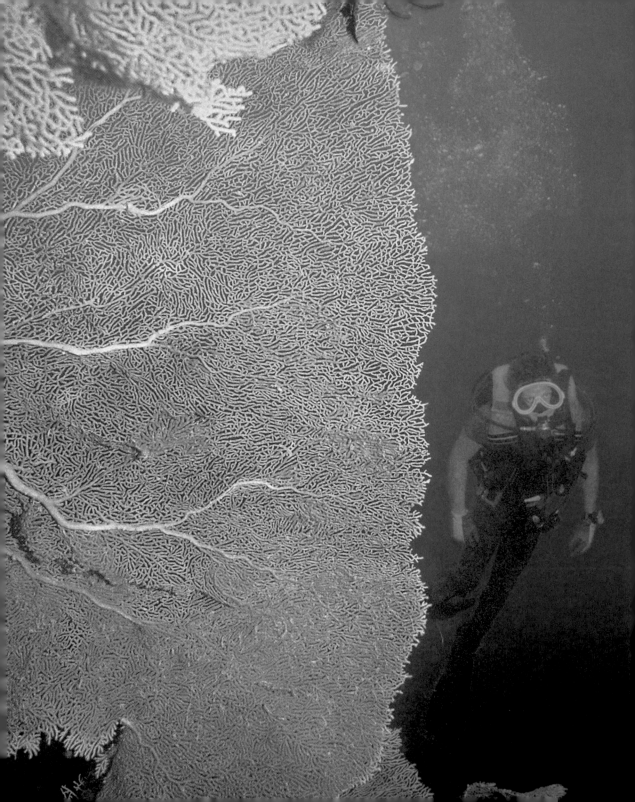

The Variety of Corals

The corals that form stony reefs are called stony corals. They tend to be drab yellow, brown, or green. That is because the algae they contain in their bodies are also drab. But coral reefs can also be tremendously colorful. That is because another type of coral lives on and among the stony corals, called octocorals. There are thousands of kinds of octocorals. Each kind is a different color. Some are vivid yellows. Some are deep purples. Some are bright pink. Some are rich blue.

Octocorals do not have a stony skeleton like stony corals, although many have a stiff, horny skeleton. Octocorals called soft corals feel rubbery, leathery, or prickly, but they are easily damaged if touched. The sea fans that are common off Florida and in the Caribbean are a kind of octocoral. Sea pens, which look like old-fashioned quill pens, are also octocorals. So are the beautiful blue corals of the Indian Ocean.

Opposite page: Sea fans are huge soft corals that look like giant fans as they waft to and fro in the water.

Corals of the Deep

Most corals live in warm, shallow seas around tropical coasts. But some do live in deep and cold water. Some also live on the seabed far from land. Deep-sea explorers have found a kind of coral reef on the cold seabed of the North Atlantic Ocean 350–750 feet (150–250 meters) down. It is very dark this deep. So the coral reefs here are nothing like tropical reefs. The corals cannot use sunlight to make sugars. They catch bits of food with their fingerlike tentacles.

Divers working for oil companies often find pale corals looking like cauliflowers growing at the base of oil-rig legs. It seems there are even corals that live in the deepest parts of the ocean. Divers have found corals in canyons in the deep ocean floor 20,000 feet (6 kilometers) down. There the water is pitch black and almost as cold as ice.

Not all corals live in shallow water. These tree corals are living deep down in the dark on the seabed.

When corals are ready to start new colonies, they release clouds of spawn into the water.

Sea of Eggs

Coral colonies normally grow as more and more polyps form. Polyps make new individuals by simply dividing in two, or by budding. Budding means a new tiny polyp appears on the side of an old one and grows like a bud on a plant. Many colonies can keep on growing for centuries by budding.

But colonies can't go on budding forever. So they continually try to start new colonies by making eggs and sperm. Corals release eggs and sperm into the ocean over a few days each spring. The release of eggs and sperm is called spawning. A coral spawning looks like an underwater, upside-down snowstorm. The billions of eggs and sperm form a scum on the ocean surface for miles around.

Each kind of coral spawns on the same day, even though the colonies might be hundreds of miles apart. With so many eggs floating around, egg-eating animals, such as crabs and seagulls, cannot finish them all. So some eggs are sure to survive and grow into young corals.

Growing Up on a Reef

When a young coral hatches from its egg, it is called a larva. The larva may swim around for only a few days after hatching. Then it looks for a place to settle down for the rest of its life. Finding a place to attach to on the reef is not easy, because the reef is already crowded with corals and other sea creatures. Indeed, coral larvae make an ideal snack for adult corals. The larva must steer well clear of them as it swims. If it settles too close to a large coral, it may find itself on the menu!

The little larva is not alone in its task, though. Some rocks are covered in seaweed that is not soft but hard and stony. Grazing parrotfish help coral larvae by scraping away the stony seaweeds from rock as they eat. A coral larva can gain a foothold on one of the bare patches of rock created by parrotfish.

Dangers of the Reef

Corals have stingers and often rock-hard armor too. But they are sitting targets for attackers because they cannot run away. Some animals, such as some clams, snails, and sponges, tunnel into a coral's rocky skeleton. They bore into a dead part of the coral colony far from the living polyp's stinging tentacles. They don't hurt the coral, but they might weaken its base so it topples over and dies.

Some animals even attack the dangerous stinging active part of the coral (the living polyps) for food. Butterfly fish have narrow, pointed snouts that they can poke into holes in the coral skeleton to get at the polyps. Parrotfish are mainly vegetarian and they eat the algae that live around and inside the coral. Many polyps die as parrotfish break off chunks of coral with their strong beaks. The worst enemy of corals by far, though, is the crown-of-thorns starfish. It crawls over corals and forces its stomach out of its mouth to smother and eat the polyps.

Opposite page: *This sunset butterfly fish looks beautiful. But for corals it is very dangerous. It has a long snout. It can poke right inside a coral's skeleton to eat the polyps.*

Jewelry and Mining

Opposite page:
Coral is such an attractive material that people have long used it to make jewelry and sculpture. This head of a god was carved from coral in the Solomon Islands in the southwest Pacific Ocean.

Some coral skeletons are so attractive that people make jewelry from them by cutting and polishing it. In the Mediterranean Sea they make jewelry from red coral, an octocoral. Elsewhere they use the thorny skeleton of black coral.

Stony coral can also be a valuable source of rock. Some coral reefs are dug out for rock. The living corals sit on a thick base of limestone created from coral skeletons over thousands of years. Limestone is a good building rock. So coral diggers remove what they can and cart away the rubble to make roads and buildings.

Jewelry making and quarrying can be a tragedy for coral reefs. Reefs take thousands of years to build up again. Once the coral reef is gone, so are all the creatures that lived on it.

In many places around the world coral is dying off, often as a result of human activity.

Pollution and Mud

Coral reefs seem to be in crisis at the moment. One-tenth of all coral reefs have been damaged beyond repair. A further one-third of all coral reefs are looking very unhealthy.

Corals can be damaged not only by people taking bits off but by changes far away, too. One damaging change is when farmers use chemical fertilizers on fields. The chemicals they use may wash into rivers and out to sea, creating pollution. The chemicals encourage plankton and algae to grow. The algae then crowd out the coral, and the plankton make the water murky, blocking out the coral's sunlight.

Another damaging change is when loggers cut down forests. When that happens, soil may be washed into rivers and into the ocean. Here, like plankton, it turns the water murky and blocks out the precious sunlight. Sometimes a flow of mud from a river buries corals alive.

Coral Bleaching

When corals are stressed, they often lose the tiny algae that normally live inside their body. It is the algae that give stony corals their color. Corals without algae look white because their pale limestone skeleton can be seen. People call this coral bleaching. When corals bleach, they sometimes get back their algae and recover. But often the corals just die.

During the 1980s and again in 1998 there was a lot of coral bleaching around the world. Perhaps three-quarters of the rich corals around Indonesia were bleached and died, for example. All this coral bleaching and death seem to have been caused by a sudden warming of the ocean. Experts don't know why the oceans got warmer. But many fear that it is because pollution caused by people is making all the Earth steadily warmer. If so, many more corals will die in the future.

*When corals are under stress, they lose the algae
that live in them and so lose their color.*

Fish, Dynamite, and Poison

In many places people catch far too many fish from coral reefs. These fish feed on algae and keep them in check. When the fish are lost, the algae grow thickly and take over, swamping the corals. This has happened on most reefs in the Caribbean.

When fish become rare, fishers also become desperate and change to extreme methods of fishing. A common way of fishing in Southeast Asia is blast fishing. Fishers drop explosives such as dynamite into the water. The explosion kills or stuns all the wildlife, and fishers collect the few fish that float to the top. But the blast also blows up coral and kills reefs.

Other fishers use poison, such as cyanide, which is squirted into coral crevices. The poison kills the coral, but only stuns fish. The fish partly recover, and aquarium keepers and restaurants then buy them.

Opposite page: People wreck corals for many reasons. This man is breaking off bits of coral to use for building.

Snorkeling and Diving

Despite all the damage to coral reefs caused by people, there is some hope for the future. More and more people are interested in visiting coral reefs and admiring them by snorkeling and diving. However, careless divers can damage coral reefs by trampling or scraping them. Coral polyps are very fragile, and one contact can kill them.

But interest in coral reefs helps protect them. Visitors coming to see coral reefs bring lots of money to spend, so local people try to protect the reefs for everyone to enjoy. Tourist money spent in hotels and on diving trips supports the people of islands such as the Maldives, the Seychelles, and the Bahamas. Coral reefs are beginning to form part of nature reserves, so some of the spectacular beauty of coral should survive.

Words to Know

Alga (plural **algae**) A simple, plantlike life form.

Bleaching Coral whitening due to the loss of the algae in its body.

Colony A group of animals living closely together.

Cyanide A deadly poison that is used by fishers to catch coral-reef fish.

Larva (plural **larvae**) The young form of an animal such as a coral.

Mineral Salty substance that is sometimes an invisible part of seawater and sometimes a part of rocks.

Paralyzed Unable to move.

Pollution Occurs when a substance damages the environment because there is too much of it, or it is in the wrong place.

Plankton Tiny animals that drift on ocean currents.

Polyp A simple individual that makes up corals.

Reef A ridge in the seabed, often built by coral.

Silt Fine mud.

Skeleton The strong part of an animal that keeps the animal from becoming floppy.

Spawn To release eggs and sperm.

Tentacle A long, bendy organ used for grasping or feeling.

INDEX

Cover Photo: Still Pictures: Rafel Al Ma'ray
Photo Credits: Ardea: K. Amsler 44, D. Parer & F. Parer-Cook 24/25, Ron & Valerie Taylor 7, 12, 31, 40; Bruce Coleman: Pacific Stock 27,35; Corbis: Stephen Frink 16; Digital Stock: 19; Jeff Jeffords: 28; NHPA: A.N.T. 32, Pete Atkinson 20, G. I. Bernard 11; Oxford Scientific Films: Schneidermeyer 39, Mark Webster 15; Still Pictures: J. Kassanchuk/UNEP 4, Pascal Kobeh 43, Jeffrey Rotman 8, Secret Sea Visions 36.